Collins

irst

ch

IARY

East
Renfrewshire
COUNCIL

Return this item by
the last date shown.

Items may be renewed
by telephone or at
www.eastrenfrewshire.gov.uk/libraries

Collins

HarperCollins Publishers

Westerhill Road
Bishopbriggs
Glasgow
G64 2QT
Great Britain

First Edition 2009

Reprint 10 9 8 7 6 5 4 3 2 1 0

© HarperCollins Publishers 2009

ISBN 978-0-00-730900-9

Collins® is a registered trademark of HarperCollins
Publishers Limited

www.collinslanguage.com

A catalogue record of this book is available from the
British Library

Printed and bound in China by South China Printing
Co., Ltd

Acknowledgements
We would like to thank those authors and
publishers who kindly gave permission for copyright
material to be used in the Collins Word Web. We
would also like to thank the Times Newspapers Ltd
for providing valuable data.

When you buy a Collins dictionary or thesaurus
and register on www.collinslanguage.com for the
free online and digital services, you will not be
charged by HarperCollins for access to Collins free
Online Dictionary content or Collins free Online
Thesaurus content on that website. However, your
operator's charges for using the internet will apply.
Costs vary from operator to operator. HarperCollins
is not responsible for any charges levied by online
service providers for accessing Collins free Online
Dictionary or Collins free Online Thesaurus on
www.collinslanguage.com using these services.

HarperCollins does not warrant that the functions
contained in www.collinslanguage.com content
will be uninterrupted or error free, that defects will
be corrected, or that www.collinslanguage.com or
the server that makes it available are free of viruses
or bugs. HarperCollins is not responsible for any
access difficulties that may be experienced due
to problems with network, web, online or mobile
phone connections.

SERIES EDITOR
Rob Scriven

MANAGING EDITOR
Gaëlle Amiot-Cadey

PROJECT MANAGEMENT
Susie Beattie
Genevieve Gerrard

DESIGN
Q2AMedia
Rob Payne

ILLUSTRATION AND IMAGE RESEARCH
Q2AMedia

Contents

a

adult
l'**adulte** *m/f*

after
après
after lunch
après le déjeuner

afternoon
l'**après-midi** *m/f*
at three o'clock in the
afternoon
à trois heures de
l'après-midi

again
encore une
fois
Try again!
Essaie encore
une fois!

airport
l'**aéroport** *m*

alien
l'**extra-**
terrestre *m*

alphabet
l'**alphabet** *m*

ambulance
l'**ambulance** *f*

and
et
my brother
and *me*
mon frère
et *moi*

animal
l'**animal** *m*
(les animaux *pl*)

apple
la **pomme**

arm
le **bras**

ask
demander à
Ask somebody.
Demande à quelqu'un.

b

balloon
le **ballon**

banana
la **banane**

baby
le **bébé**

basket
le **panier**

bad
mauvais,
mauvaise
bad weather
*le **mauvais** temps*

bath
le **bain**

bag
le **sac**

beach
la **plage**

ball
le **ballon**

bed
le **lit**

bedroom
la **chambre**

before
avant
before three o'clock
avant trois heures

bicycle
le **vélo**

big
grand, grande
*a **big** house*
*une **grande** maison*

blanket
la couverture

book
le livre

bird
l'oiseau *m*
(les oiseaux *pl*)

blue
bleu, bleue
*a **blue** dress*
*une robe **bleue***

boot
la botte

birthday
l'anniversaire *m*

boat
le bateau
(les bateaux *pl*)

box
la boîte

boy
le garçon

body
le corps

black
noir, noire
*a **black** car*
*une voiture **noire***

bread
le **pain**

brother
le **frère**

butter
le **beurre**

breakfast
le **petit déjeuner**

bucket
le **seau**
(les seaux *pl*)

butterfly
le **papillon**

bridge
le **pont**

burger
le **hamburger**

bring
apporter

*Could you **bring** me
a glass of water?*

*Tu peux m'**apporter**
un verre d'eau?*

bus
le **bus**

buy
acheter

*She's **buying** bread.*
*Elle **achète** du pain.*

C

candle
la **bougie**

castle
le **château**
(les châteaux *pl*)

cap
la **casquette**

cake
le **gâteau**
(les gâteaux *pl*)

car
la **voiture**

cat
le **chat**

calendar
le **calendrier**

card
la **carte**

chair
la **chaise**

carpet
la **moquette**

cheese
le **fromage**

call
appeler

Call this number.
Appelle ce numéro.

chicken
le **poulet**

carrot
la **carotte**

child
l'**enfant** m/f

circle
le **cercle**

clock
le **réveil**

clothes
les **vêtements** mpl

circus
le **cirque**

chocolate
le **chocolat**

cloud
le **nuage**

classroom
la **classe**

chopsticks
les **baguettes** fpl

cinema
le **cinéma**

clean
propre
a **clean** shirt
une chemise **propre**

clown
le **clown**

coat
le **manteau**
(les manteaux *pl*)

computer
l'**ordinateur** *m*

cow
la **vache**

coffee
le **café**

cook
cuisiner
I can **cook**.
Je sais **cuisiner**.

cry
pleurer
Why **are** *you* **crying**?
Pourquoi tu **pleures**?

cold
**froid,
froide**
The water's **cold**.
L'eau est **froide**.

costume
le **costume**

curtain
le **rideau**
(les rideaux *pl*)

come
venir
Come *with me.*
Viens *avec moi.*

countryside
la **campagne**

a
b
c
d
e
f
g
h
i
j
k
l
m
n
o
p
q
r
s
t
u
v
w
x
y
z

dad
le **papa**

daughter
la **fille**

day
le **jour**
*What **day** is it today?*
*Quel **jour** sommes-nous?*

dinner
le **dîner**

dinosaur
le **dinosaure**

dance
danser
*I like **dancing**.*
*J'aime **danser**.*

dessert
le **dessert**

dirty
sale
*My shoes are **dirty**.*
*Mes chaussures sont **sales**.*

dictionary
le **dictionnaire**

dangerous
dangereux,
dangereuse
*It's **dangerous**!*
*C'est **dangereux**!*

do
faire
*What **are** you **doing**?*
*Qu'est-ce que tu **fais**?*

difficult
difficile
*It's **difficult**.*
*C'est **difficile**.*

a b c **d** e f g h i j k l m n o p q r s t u v w x y z

doctor
le **médecin**

door
la **porte**

dream
le **rêve**

dog
le **chien**

downstairs
en bas
*I'm **downstairs**!*
*Je suis **en bas**!*

dress
la **robe**

doll
la **poupée**

drink
boire
***Drink** your milk.*
***Bois** ton lait.*

dragon
le **dragon**

dolphin
le **dauphin**

draw
dessiner
***Draw** a house.*
***Dessine** une maison.*

duck
le **canard**

DVD
le **DVD**

a b c **d** e f g h i j k l m n o p q r s t u v w x y z

e

egg
l'**œuf** m

evening
le **soir**
at six o'clock in the **evening**
à six heures du **soir**

elephant
l'**éléphant** m

every
tout,
toute
(tous *pl*)
every day
tous les jours

ear
l'**oreille** f

Earth
la **Terre**

email
le **mail**

easy
facile
It's **easy**!
C'est **facile**!

exercise
l'**exercice** m

eat
manger
I **eat** a lot of sweets.
Je **mange** beaucoup
de bonbons.

empty
vide
The bottle is **empty**.
La bouteille est **vide**.

eye
l'**œil** m
(les yeux *pl*)

a
b
c
d
e
f
g
h
i
j
k
l
m
n
o
p
q
r
s
t
u
v
w
x
y
z

11

f

father
le **père**

fire
le **feu**
(les feux *pl*)

face
la **figure**

favourite
préféré,
préférée
*Blue's my **favourite** colour.*
*Ma couleur **préférée**,*
c'est le bleu.

fireworks
le **feu**
d'artifice

fairy
la **fée**

find
trouver
*I can't **find** my bag.*
*Je ne **trouve** plus mon sac.*

first
premier,
première
*the **first** day*
*le **premier** jour*

family
la **famille**

fast
vite
*You walk **fast**.*
*Tu marches **vite**.*

finger
le **doigt**

fish
le **poisson**

floor
*Sit **on the floor**.*
*Assieds-toi **par terre**.*

forest
la **forêt**

from
de
*a letter **from** my friend*
*une lettre **de** mon ami*

flower
la **fleur**

fork
la **fourchette**

fruit
le **fruit**

fly
la **mouche**

fridge
le **frigo**

food
la **nourriture**

full
plein,
pleine
*The bottle's **full**.*
*La bouteille est **pleine**.*

friend
l'**ami** *m,*
l'**amie** *f*

football
le **football**

funny
drôle
*It's very **funny**.*
*C'est très **drôle**.*

frog
la **grenouille**

a
b
c
d
e
f
g
h
i
j
k
l
m
n
o
p
q
r
s
t
u
v
w
x
y
z

g

ghost
le **fantôme**

**give
donner**
Give me the book, please.
Donne-moi le livre,
s'il te plaît.

game
le **jeu**
(les jeux *pl*)

giant
le **géant**

garage
le **garage**

glass
le **verre**

giraffe
la **girafe**

glasses
les **lunettes** *fpl*

glove
le **gant**

garden
le **jardin**

girl
la **fille**

glue
la **colle**

go
aller
*Where **are** you **going**?*
*Où **vas**-tu?*

goodbye
au revoir!

grow
grandir
*Haven't you **grown**!*
*Comme tu **as grandi**!*

goat
la chèvre

grapes
le raisin

guinea pig
le cochon d'Inde

grass
l'herbe *f*

goldfish
le poisson rouge

ground
*We sat on the **ground**.*
*Nous nous sommes assis par **terre**.*

guitar
la guitare

good
bon, bonne
*That's a **good** idea.*
*C'est une **bonne** idée.*

h

happy
heureux, heureuse
*She is **happy**.*
*Elle est **heureuse**.*

head
la tête

hair
les cheveux mpl
*He's got black **hair**.*
*Il a les **cheveux** noirs.*

hairdresser
le coiffeur,
la coiffeuse

hear
entendre
*I can't **hear** you.*
*Je ne t'**entends** pas.*

hard
dur,
dure
*This cheese is very **hard**.*
*Ce fromage est très **dur**.*

hedgehog
le hérisson

helicopter
l'hélicoptère m

hamster
le hamster

hat
le chapeau
(les chapeaux *pl*)

hello
bonjour!

hand
la main

have
avoir
*I **have** a bike.*
*J'**ai** un vélo.*

a b c d e f g h i j k l m n o p q r s t u v w x y z

here
ici
*I live **here**.*
*J'habite **ici**.*

hide
se cacher
*She's **hiding** under the bed.*
*Elle **se cache** sous le lit.*

holiday
les vacances *fpl*
*We're on **holiday**.*
*Nous sommes en **vacances**.*

homework
les devoirs *mpl*

horse
le cheval
(les chevaux *pl*)

hospital
l'hôpital *m*
(les hôpitaux *pl*)

hot
chaud,
chaude
*a hot **bath***
*un bain **chaud***

hour
l'heure *f*

house
la maison

hungry
*I'm **hungry**.*
J'ai faim.

hurry up
***Hurry up**, children!*
***Dépêchez-vous**, les enfants!*

husband
le mari

i

j

jigsaw
le **puzzle**

ice cream
la **glace**

jacket
la **veste**

job
le **travail**

idea
l'**idée** *f*

juice
le **jus**

*I'd like some orange **juice**.*
*Je voudrais du **jus** d'orange.*

jam
la **confiture**

insect
l'**insecte** *m*

island
l'**île** *f*

jeans
le **jean**

jump
sauter

Jump!
Saute!

18

k

keep
garder
*You can **keep** the book.*
*Tu peux **garder** le livre.*

key
la **clé**

kid
le/la **gosse** *m/f*

kind
gentil,
gentille
*a **kind** person*
*une personne **gentille***

king
le **roi**

kiss
le **bisou**
*Give me a **kiss**.*
*Fais-moi un **bisou**.*

kitchen
la **cuisine**

kite
le **cerf-volant**

kitten
le **chaton**

knee
le **genou**
(les genoux *pl*)

knife
le **couteau**
(les couteaux *pl*)

know
savoir
*I don't **know**.*
*Je ne **sais** pas.*

a b c d e f g h i j **k** l m n o p q r s t u v w x y z

l

laptop
le **portable**

leg
la **jambe**

lady
la **dame**

late
en retard
*I'm **late** for school.*
*Je suis **en retard**
pour l'école.*

lemon
le **citron**

less
moins
*I've got **less** than him!*
*J'en ai **moins** que lui!*

lake
le **lac**

laugh
rire
*Why **are** you **laughing**?*
*Pourquoi tu **ris**?*

lamb
l'**agneau** *m*
(les agneaux *pl*)

letter
la **lettre**

learn
apprendre
*I'**m learning** to dance.*
*J'**apprends** à danser.*

lamp
la **lampe**

light
la **lumière**

20

like
aimer
*I **like** cherries.*
*J'**aime** les cerises.*

lion
le lion

listen
écouter
***Listen** to me!*
***Écoute**-moi!*

little
petit, petite
*a **little** girl*
*une **petite** fille*

live
habiter
*I **live** here.*
*J'**habite** ici.*

look
regarder
***Look at** the picture.*
***Regarde** cette image.*

lose
perdre
*I'**ve lost** my purse.*
*J'**ai perdu** mon porte-monnaie.*

lost
perdu, perdue
*I'm **lost**.*
*Je suis **perdu**.*

loud
fort, forte
*It's too **loud**.*
*C'est trop **fort**.*

love
aimer
*I **love** you.*
*Je t'**aime**.*

lucky
*You're **lucky**!*
Tu as de la chance!

lunch
le déjeuner

m

many
beaucoup de
*He hasn't got **many** friends.*
*Il n'a pas **beaucoup**
d'amis.*

meet
rencontrer
*I **met** my friend in town.*
*J'**ai rencontré** mon amie
en ville.*

magician
le **magicien**

market
le **marché**

meal
le **repas**

mermaid
la **sirène**

make
faire
*I'm going to **make** a cake.*
*Je vais **faire** un gâteau.*

meat
la **viande**

mess
le **bazar**

man
l'**homme** m

medicine
le **médicament**

milk
le **lait**

a b c d e f g h i j k l **m** n o p q r s t u v w x y z

money
l'**argent** *m*

monkey
le **singe**

monster
le **monstre**

month
le **mois**
*What **month** is it?*
*Quel **mois** sommes-nous?*

moon
la **lune**

more
plus de
*There are **more** girls than boys.*
*Il y a **plus de** filles que de garçons.*

morning
le **matin**
*at seven o'clock in the **morning***
*à sept heures du **matin***

mother
la **mère**

motorbike
la **moto**

mountain
la **montagne**

mouse
la **souris**

mouth
la **bouche**

mum
la **maman**

music
la **musique**

n

name
le **nom**

need
avoir besoin de
*I **need** a rubber.*
*J'**ai besoin d'**une gomme.*

neighbour
le **voisin**,
la **voisine**

newspaper
le **journal**
(les journaux *pl*)

next
prochain,
prochaine
*The **next** street on the left.*
*La **prochaine** rue à gauche.*

nice
gentil,
gentille
*He's **nice**.*
*Il est **gentil**.*

night
la **nuit**

noise
le **bruit**

nose
le **nez**
(les nez *pl*)

nothing
rien
*He does **nothing**.*
*Il ne fait **rien**.*

now
maintenant
*Do it **now**!*
*Fais-le
maintenant!*

number
le **numéro**

nurse
l'**infirmier** *m*,
l'**infirmière** *f*

of
de
*some photos **of** my family*
*des photos **de** ma famille*

old
vieux,
vieille
*an **old** dog*
*un **vieux** chien*

only
seul,
seule
*my **only** dress*
*ma **seule** robe*

open
ouvrir
*Can I **open** the window?*
*Est-ce que je peux **ouvrir** la fenêtre?*

other
autre
*on the **other** side of the street*
*de l'**autre** côté de la rue*

page
la page

paint
peindre
*I'm going to **paint** it green.*
*Je vais le **peindre** en vert.*

paper
le papier

parents
les **parents** *mpl*

passport
le **passeport**

pasta
les **pâtes** *fpl*

people
les **gens** *mpl*

park
le **parc**

pet
l'**animal** *m*
(les animaux *pl*)

peas
les **petits pois** *mpl*

photo
la **photo**

party
la **fête**

pen
le **stylo**

pencil
le **crayon**

piano
le **piano**

picnic
le **pique-nique**

plane
l'**avion** *m*

pocket
la **poche**

plant
la **plante**

pocket money
l'**argent de poche** *m*

picture
le **dessin**

plate
l'**assiette** *f*

play
jouer
I **play** tennis.
Je **joue** au tennis.

police
la **police**

pirate
le **pirate**

playground
l'**aire de jeux** *f*

pony
le **poney**

pizza
la **pizza**

a b c d e f g h i j k l m n o **p** q r s t u v w x y z

27

postcard
la **carte postale**

pretty
joli,
jolie
a *pretty* dress
une *jolie* robe

puppet
la **marionnette**

postman
le **facteur**

prince
le **prince**

puppy
le **chiot**

pushchair
la **poussette**

potato
la **pomme**
de terre

princess
la **princesse**

pyjamas
le **pyjama**

present
le **cadeau**
(les cadeaux *pl*)

q

r

rainbow
l'**arc-en-ciel** m

queen
la **reine**

quick
rapide

a **quick** lunch
un déjeuner **rapide**

quiet
tranquille

a **quiet** little town
une petite ville **tranquille**

rabbit
le **lapin**

race
la **course**

radio
la **radio**

rain
la **pluie**

read
lire

I **read** a lot.
Je **lis** beaucoup.

ready
prêt,
prête

Breakfast is **ready**.
Le petit déjeuner est **prêt**.

red
rouge

a **red** T-shirt
un tee-shirt **rouge**

remember
se souvenir de
I can't remember his name.
Je ne me souviens pas de son nom.

right
bon,
bonne
It isn't the right size.
Ce n'est pas la bonne taille.

robot
le **robot**

rocket
la **fusée**

restaurant
le **restaurant**

ring
la **bague**

river
la **rivière**

room
la **pièce**

rice
le **riz**

rich
riche
He's very rich.
Il est très riche.

road
la **route**

run
courir
Run!
Cours!

a b c d e f g h i j k l m n o p q r s t u v w x y z

30

S

sandwich
le sandwich

say
dire
*What **did** you **say**?*
*Qu'est-ce que tu **as dit**?*

second
deuxième

sad
triste
*Don't be **sad**.*
*Ne sois pas **triste**.*

school
l'école *f*

see
voir
*I **can see** her car.*
*Je **vois** sa voiture.*

same
même
*They're in the **same** class.*
*Ils sont dans la **même** classe.*

scissors
les ciseaux *mpl*

sell
vendre
*He's **selling** his bike.*
*Il **vend** son vélo.*

sand
le sable

sea
la mer

a b c d e f g h i j k l m n o p q r s t u v w x y z

send
envoyer
Send me an email.
Envoie-moi un mail.

shadow
l'ombre f

sheep
le mouton

shirt
la chemise

shoe
la chaussure

shop
le magasin

shorts
le short

shout
crier
Don't **shout**, children!
Ne **criez** pas, les enfants!

show
montrer
Show me the photos.
Montre-moi les photos.

shower
la douche

sick
malade
He is **sick**.
Il est **malade**.

sing
chanter
I **sing** in the choir.
Je **chante** dans la chorale.

sister
la sœur

sit
s'asseoir
*Can I **sit** here?*
*Je peux **m'asseoir** ici?*

skin
la peau

skirt
la jupe

sky
le ciel

sleep
dormir
*My cat **sleeps** in a box.*
*Mon chat **dort** dans une boîte.*

slow
lent, lente
*The tortoise is very **slow**.*
*La tortue est très **lente**.*

smell
sentir
*Mmm, that **smells** good!*
*Mmm, ça **sent** bon!*

smile
le sourire

snail
l'escargot m

snake
le serpent

snow
la neige

snowman
le bonhomme de neige

soap
le savon

a
b
c
d
e
f
g
h
i
j
k
l
m
n
o
p
q
r
s
t
u
v
w
x
y
z

33

sock
la **chaussette**

soup
la **soupe**

spoon
la **cuillère**

sofa
le **canapé**

spaceship
le **vaisseau spatial**

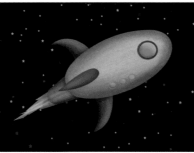

sport
le **sport**

square
le **carré**

son
le **fils**

speak
parler

*Do you **speak** English?*
*Est-ce que tu **parles** anglais?*

stairs
l'**escalier** m

sorry
pardon!

spider
l'**araignée** f

star
l'**étoile** f

station
la gare

stick
coller
Stick it onto the paper.
Colle-le sur le papier.

sticker
l'autocollant *m*

stone
la pierre

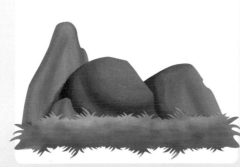

stop
arrêter
Stop, that's enough!
Arrête, ça suffit!

story
l'histoire *f*

street
la rue

strong
fort,
forte
She's very strong.
Elle est très forte.

sun
le soleil

supermarket
le supermarché

surprise
la surprise
What a surprise!
Quelle surprise!

swim
nager
I can swim.
Je sais nager.

swimming
pool
la piscine

t

tall
haut,
haute
*a very **tall** building*
*un très **haut** immeuble*

telephone
le **téléphone**

table
la **table**

television
la **télévision**

take
prendre
Take *a card.*
Prends *une carte.*

taxi
le **taxi**

text message
le **SMS**

tea
le **thé**

talk
parler
*You **talk** too much.*
*Tu **parles** trop.*

teddy bear
le **nounours**

thank you
merci!

36

think
penser
*What **are** you **thinking**
about?*
*À quoi tu **penses**?*

third
troisième
*the **third** prize*
*le **troisième** prix*

tie
la **cravate**

tiger
le **tigre**

tired
fatigué,
fatiguée
*I'm **tired**.*
*Je suis **fatigué**.*

toast
le **pain grillé**

today
aujourd'hui
*It's Monday **today**.*
***Aujourd'hui** c'est lundi.*

together
ensemble

toilet
les **toilettes** *fpl*

tomato
la **tomate**

tomorrow
demain
*See you **tomorrow**!*
*À **demain**!*

tooth
la **dent**

toothbrush
la **brosse à**
dents

toothpaste
le **dentifrice**

toy
le **jouet**

tree
l'**arbre** m

tortoise
la **tortue**

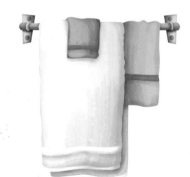

tractor
le **tracteur**

triangle
le **triangle**

towel
la **serviette**

train
le **train**

trousers
le **pantalon**

town
la **ville**

treasure
le **trésor**

T-shirt
le **tee-shirt**

a b c d e f g h i j k l m n o p q r s **t** u v w x y z

u

up
en haut
*The cat is **up** on the roof.*
*Le chat est **en haut** sur le toit.*

very
très
very small
très petit

umbrella
le parapluie

upstairs
en haut

vet
le/la
vétérinaire *m/f*

understand
comprendre
*I don't **understand**.*
*Je ne **comprends** pas.*

video game
le jeu vidéo

v

uniform
l'uniforme *m*

vanilla
la vanille
vanilla ice cream
*la glace à la **vanille***

vegetable
le légume

visit
visiter
*We're going to **visit** the castle.*
*Nous allons **visiter** le château.*

a
b
c
d
e
f
g
h
i
j
k
l
m
n
o
p
q
r
s
t
u
v
w
x
y
z

W

wall
le mur
There are posters on the wall.
Il y a des posters au mur.

watch
la montre

water
l'eau *f*

wait
attendre
Wait for me!
Attends-moi!

want
vouloir
Do you want some cake?
Tu veux du gâteau?

wave
la vague

wake up
se réveiller
Wake up!
Réveille-toi!

warm
chaud, chaude
warm water
l'eau chaude

wear
porter
He's wearing a hat.
Il porte un chapeau.

walk
marcher
He walks fast.
Il marche vite.

wash
se laver
Wash your hands!
Lave-toi les mains!

webcam
la webcam

website
le **site web**

well
bien
*She played **well**.*
*Elle a **bien** joué.*

wild
sauvage
*a **wild** animal*
*un animal **sauvage***

week
la **semaine**
*I play football every **week**.*
*Je joue au football chaque **semaine**.*

wheelchair
le **fauteuil roulant**

win
gagner
*I always **win**.*
*Je **gagne** tout le temps.*

weekend
le **week-end**
*I play tennis at the **weekend**.*
*Je joue au tennis le **week-end**.*

white
blanc, blanche
*My shirt is **white**.*
*Ma chemise est **blanche**.*

wind
le **vent**

welcome
bienvenue!

wife
la **femme**

window
la **fenêtre**

winner
le **gagnant,**
la **gagnante**

wolf
le **loup**

world
le **monde**

woman
la **femme**

write
écrire
I'm writing to my friend.
J'écris à mon ami.

witch
la **sorcière**

word
le **mot**

SNAKE   TRUCK

with
avec
Come with me.
Viens avec moi.

wrong
faux,
fausse
This answer is wrong.
Cette réponse est fausse.

work
travailler
She works in a bank.
Elle travaille dans une banque.

without
sans
without a coat
sans manteau

a
b
c
d
e
f
g
h
i
j
k
l
m
n
o
p
q
r
s
t
u
v
w
x
y
z

x

y

young
jeune
She's young.
Elle est jeune.

X-ray
la **radio**

year
l'**an** *m*
I'm seven years old.
J'ai sept ans.

z

yellow
jaune
I'm wearing
yellow *shorts.*
Je porte un
short jaune.

zebra
le **zèbre**

xylophone
le **xylophone**

yesterday
hier
I was late yesterday.
J'étais en retard hier.

zoo
le **zoo**

Les animaux
Animals

le chat
cat

le crocodile
crocodile

le zèbre
zebra

l'éléphant *m*
elephant

le serpent
snake

le pingouin
penguin

44 **la girafe**
giraffe

le loup
wolf

le lézard
lizard

le cheval
horse

la **vache**
cow

le **chien**
dog

le **lion**
lion

l'**hippopotame** *m*
hippo

le **panda**
panda

le **tigre**
tiger

l'**oiseau** *m*
bird

le **lapin**
rabbit

le **poisson**
fish

le **mouton**
sheep

le **singe**
monkey

le **kangourou**
kangaroo

45

La ville
Town

la **boulangerie**
bakery

la **banque**
bank

le **supermarché**
supermarket

la **rue**
street

le **magasin**
shop

l'**hôpital** *m*
hospital

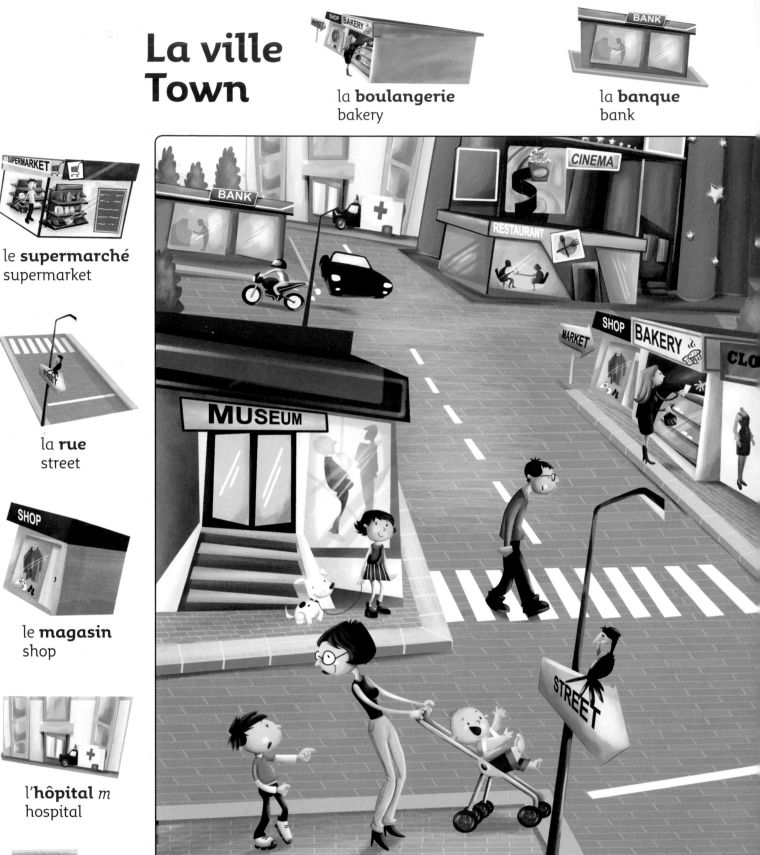

la **gare**
station

la **poste**
post office

le **parc**
park

l'**avion** *m*
plane

le **bus**
bus

le **train**
train

la **voiture**
car

le **vélo**
bicycle

le **restaurant**
restaurant

le **cinéma**
cinema

le **musée**
museum

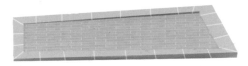

le **trottoir**
pavement

le **marché**
market

47

L'école
School

la **gomme**
rubber

le **taille-crayon**
sharpener

la **trousse**
pencil case

l'**élève** *m/f*
pupil

le **cartable**
schoolbag

la **cour de récréation**
playground

le **toboggan**
slide

le **tourniquet**
roundabout

la **balançoire**
swing

la **classe**
classroom

le **crayon**
pencil

le **stylo**
pen

le **règle**
ruler

le **cahier**
exercise book

le **poster**
poster

la **chaise**
chair

l'**ordinateur** *m*
computer

le **bureau**
desk

le **placard**
cupboard

le **tableau interactif**
interactive whiteboard

le **professeur**   49
teacher

La maison
House

le **grenier**
attic

le **garage**
garage

la **chambre**
bedroom

la **salle à manger**
dining room

la **salle de bains**
bathroom

l'**escalier** *m*
stairs

le **salon**
living room

le **toit**
roof

la **cuisine**
kitchen

le **bureau**
study

la **porte**
door

la **fenêtre**
window

le **jardin**
garden

50

La chambre
Bedroom

le **réveil**
alarm clock

le **lit**
bed

le **jouet**
toy

l'**ordinateur** m
computer

le **lecteur de CD**
CD player

la **table de chevet**
bedside table

la **commode**
chest of drawers

l'**étagère** f
bookshelf

les **rideaux** mpl
curtains

l'**armoire** f
wardrobe

la **lampe**
lamp

le **miroir**
mirror

le **pyjama**
pyjamas

l'**oreiller** m
pillow

la **couette**
duvet

les **chaussons** mpl
slippers

le **bureau**
desk

51

La nourriture
Food

les **chips** *fpl*
crisps

le **biscuit**
biscuit

l'**eau** *f*
water

l'**assiette** *f*
plate

la **tasse**
cup

le **couteau**
knife

la **fourchette**
fork

la **cuillère**
spoon

la **pomme**
apple

l'**orange** *f*
orange

les **carottes** *fpl*
carrots

la **salade**
salad

le **beurre**
butter

le **fromage**
cheese

les **frites** *fpl*
chips

la **glace**
ice cream

le **pain**
bread

le **hamburger**
burger

le **poulet**
chicken

le **jus de fruits**
fruit juice

le **lait**
milk

les **pâtes** *fpl*
pasta

le **sandwich**
sandwich

la **pizza**
pizza

le **riz**
rice

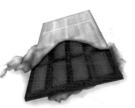
le **chocolat**
chocolate

53

Bon anniversaire!
Happy birthday!

le **gâteau**
cake

l'**amie** *f*
friend

l'**ami** *m*
friend

la **mamie**
grandma

le **papi**
granddad

les **chips** *fpl*
crisps

la **limonade**
lemonade

le **ballon**
balloon

l'**appareil photo** *m*
camera

la **bougie**
candle

le **papa**
dad

la **maman**
mum

la **sœur**
sister

le **cadeau**
present

les **bonbons** *mpl*
sweets

le **frère**
brother

55

Le corps
Body

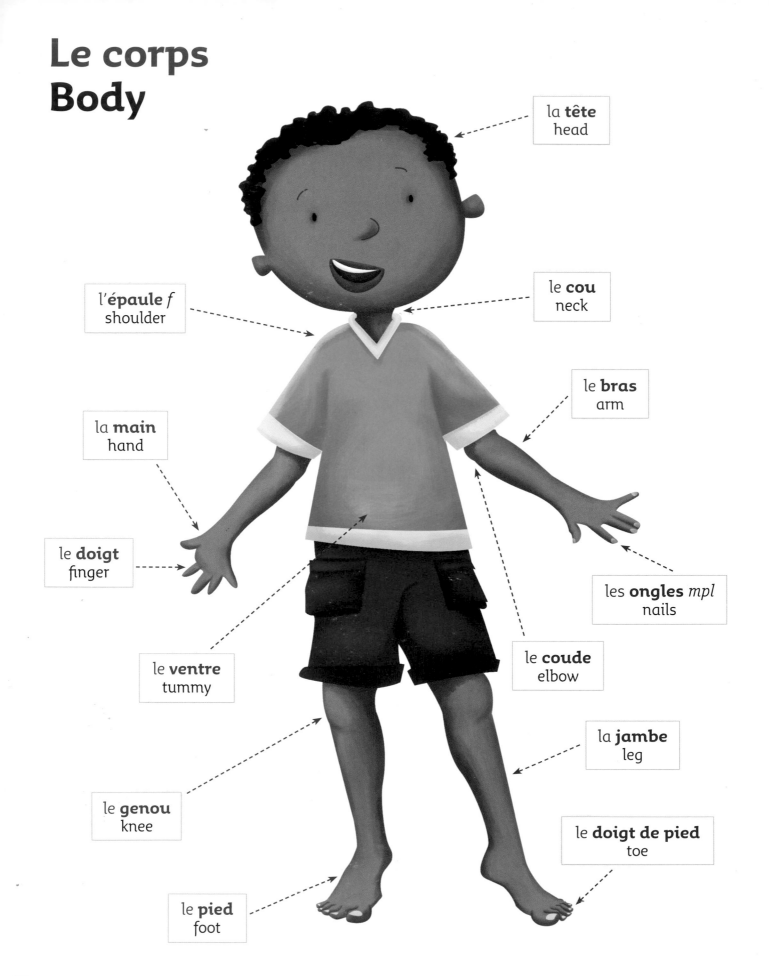

la **tête**
head

le **cou**
neck

l'**épaule** *f*
shoulder

le **bras**
arm

la **main**
hand

le **doigt**
finger

les **ongles** *mpl*
nails

le **ventre**
tummy

le **coude**
elbow

la **jambe**
leg

le **genou**
knee

le **doigt de pied**
toe

le **pied**
foot

Le visage
Face

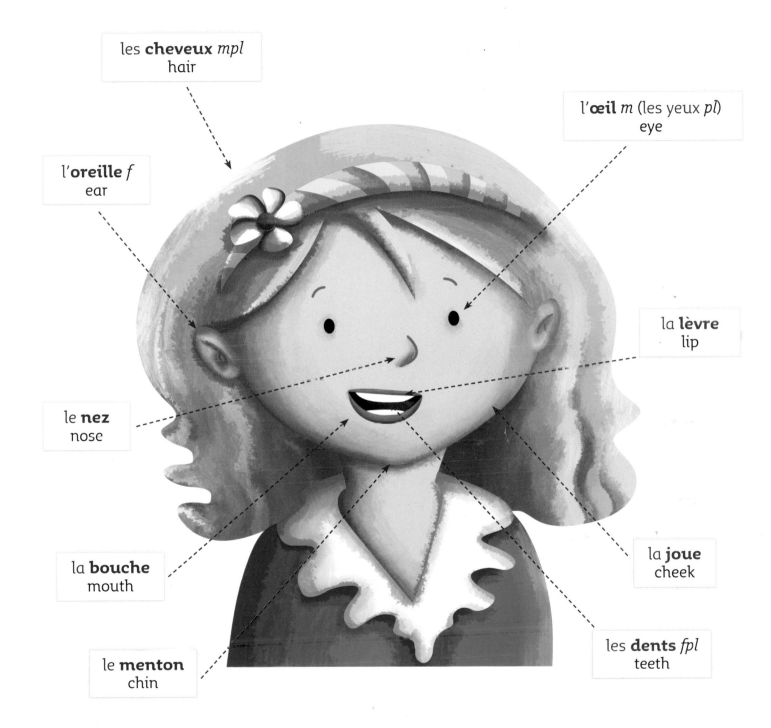

les **cheveux** *mpl*
hair

l'**oreille** *f*
ear

l'**œil** *m* (les yeux *pl*)
eye

la **lèvre**
lip

le **nez**
nose

la **joue**
cheek

la **bouche**
mouth

les **dents** *fpl*
teeth

le **menton**
chin

Les couleurs
Colours

noir, noire
black

bleu, bleue
blue

marron
brown

vert, verte
green

gris, grise
grey

bleu marine
navy

orange
orange

rose
pink

violet, violette
purple

rouge
red

blanc, blanche
white

jaune
yellow

Les vêtements
Clothes

le **sweat**
sweatshirt

la **robe**
dress

la **veste**
jacket

le **jean**
jeans

l'**écharpe** *f*
scarf

les **gants** *mpl*
gloves

le **manteau**
coat

le **pull**
jumper

les **chaussures** *fpl*
shoes

la **chemise**
shirt

les **chaussettes** *fpl*
socks

la **casquette**
cap

le **bonnet
de laine**
woolly hat

les **baskets** *fpl*
trainers

le **haut**
top

le **collant**
tights

le **pantalon**
trousers

le **tee-shirt**
T-shirt

la **jupe**
skirt

59

Les descriptions
Describing people

J'ai chaud.
I'm hot.

J'ai froid.
I'm cold.

J'ai sommeil.
I'm sleepy.

J'ai faim.
I'm hungry.

J'ai soif.
I'm thirsty.

Je suis heureuse.
I'm happy.

Je suis intelligente.
I'm intelligent.

Je suis triste.
I'm sad.

61

Les conversations
Conversations

Au revoir!
Goodbye!

Pourquoi tu pleures?
Why are you crying?

Je suis perdue.
I'm lost.

S'il te plaît!
Please!

Bonjour!
Hello!

À quelle heure commence l'école?
When does school start?

Tu as combien de frères et sœurs?
How many brothers and sisters do you have?

À neuf heures.
At nine o'clock.

J'ai un frère et deux sœurs.
I have one brother and two sisters.

Qu'est-ce que tu aimes faire?
What do you enjoy doing?

J'aime...
I like...

danser
dancing

chanter
singing

jouer de la guitare
playing guitar

jouer du piano
playing piano

jouer au foot
playing football

faire du vélo
riding my bike

jouer au basket
playing basketball

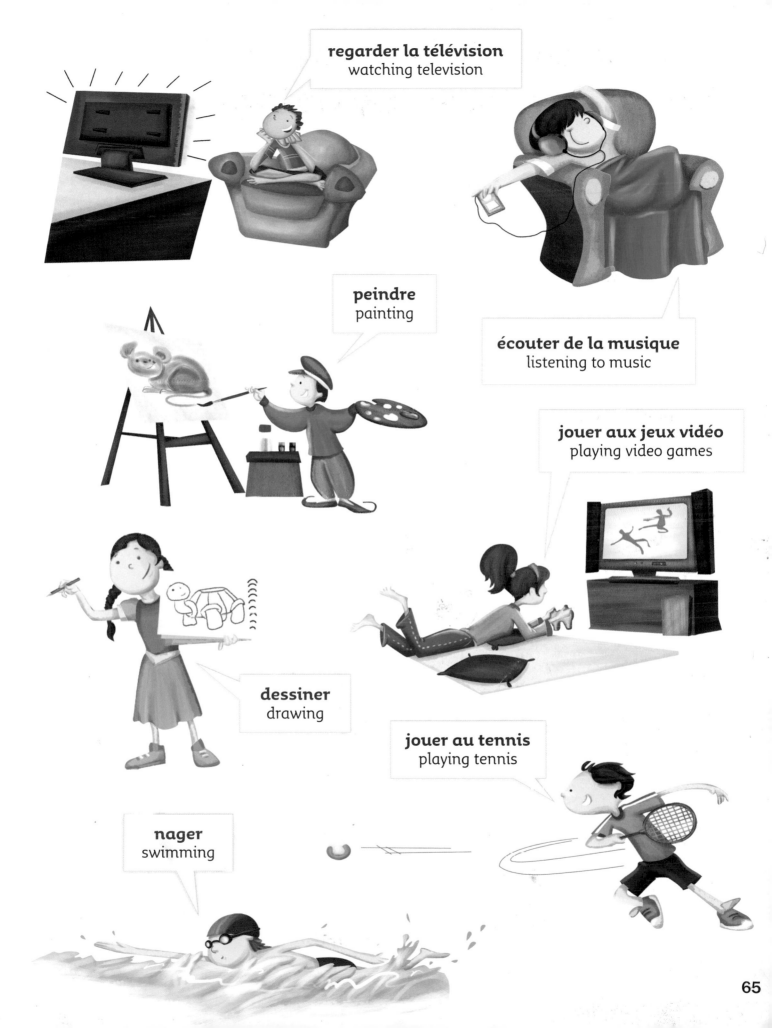

regarder la télévision
watching television

peindre
painting

écouter de la musique
listening to music

jouer aux jeux vidéo
playing video games

dessiner
drawing

jouer au tennis
playing tennis

nager
swimming

Les mois de l'année
Months of the year

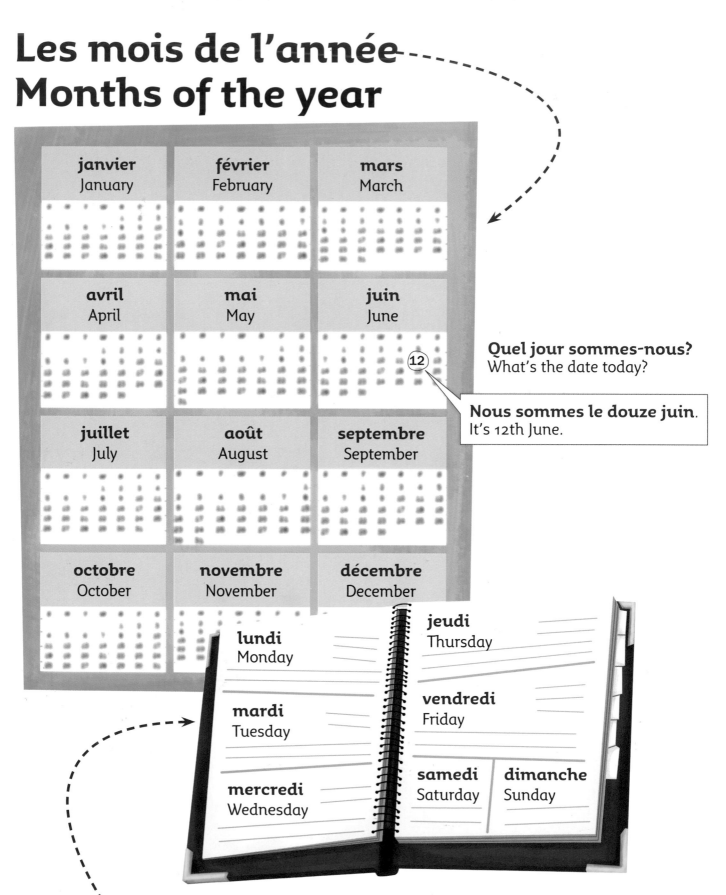

janvier January	**février** February	**mars** March
avril April	**mai** May	**juin** June
juillet July	**août** August	**septembre** September
octobre October	**novembre** November	**décembre** December

Quel jour sommes-nous?
What's the date today?

Nous sommes le douze juin.
It's 12th June.

lundi Monday

mardi Tuesday

mercredi Wednesday

jeudi Thursday

vendredi Friday

samedi Saturday

dimanche Sunday

Les jours de la semaine
Days of the week

Les saisons
Seasons

le printemps
spring

l'été *m*
summer

l'automne *m*
autumn

l'hiver *m*
winter

Quel temps fait-il?
What's the weather like?

Il fait gris.
It's cloudy.

Il fait froid.
It's cold.

Il y a du brouillard.
It's foggy.

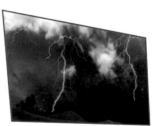
Il gèle.
It's icy.

Le ciel est couvert.
It's overcast.

Il pleut.
It's raining.

Il neige.
It's snowing.

Le temps est orageux.
It's stormy.

Il y a du vent.
It's windy.

Il fait chaud.
It's hot.

Il y a du soleil.
It's sunny.

Il fait beau.
It's nice.

Les nombres
Numbers

0 zéro	10 dix	20 vingt	80 quatre-vingts
1 un	11 onze	21 vingt et un	81 quatre-vingt-un
2 deux	12 douze	22 vingt-deux	82 quatre-vingt-deux
3 trois	13 treize	30 trente	90 quatre-vingt-dix
4 quatre	14 quatorze	40 quarante	91 quatre-vingt-onze
5 cinq	15 quinze	50 cinquante	100 cent
6 six	16 seize	60 soixante	101 cent un
7 sept	17 dix-sept	70 soixante-dix	200 deux cents
8 huit	18 dix-huit	71 soixante et onze	250 deux cent cinquante
9 neuf	19 dix-neuf	72 soixante-douze	1000 mille

Quelle heure est-il?
What's the time?

une heure
one o'clock

une heure dix
ten past one

une heure et quart
quarter past one

une heure et demie
half past one

deux heures moins vingt
twenty to two

deux heures moins le quart
quarter to two

À quelle heure...?
What time...?

à onze heures et quart
at quarter past eleven

à midi
at midday

à une heure
at one o'clock

à six heures
at six o'clock

à neuf heures moins le quart
at quarter to nine

à minuit
at midnight

69

Où sont-ils?
Where are they?

Le chien est **derrière** la télévision.
The dog is **behind** the television.

Le chat est **en haut**
sur le toit.
The cat is **up** on the roof.

La voiture est **devant**
la maison.
The car is **in front of**
the house.

La souris est **en bas**
dans la cave.
The mouse is **down**
in the cellar.

L'oiseau est **loin de**
l'arbre.
The bird is **far away**
from the tree.

L'arbre est **près de**
la maison.
The tree is **near**
the house.

Elle va **de** la maison
à l'école.
She is going **from** the
house **to** the school.

Il est **ici**.
He is **here**.

Elle est **là**.
She is **there**.

Attends-moi **dehors**.
Wait for me **outside**.

Le chat est **dans** la boîte.
The cat is **in** the box.

Il sort **du** jardin.
He is coming **out of** the garden.

Il saute **dans** la piscine.
He is jumping **into** the pool.

Elle est **à l'intérieur** de la maison.
She's **inside** the house.

La voiture tourne **à gauche**.
The car is turning **left**.

Le vélo tourne **à droite**.
The bike is turning **right**.

Le chat est **sous** la table.
The cat is **under** the table.

Le chien est **entre** les deux chats.
The dog is **between** the two cats.

La banque est **en face du** restaurant.
The bank is **opposite** the restaurant.

Le chien est **sur** le canapé.
The dog is **on** the sofa.

La boulangerie est **à côté du** supermarché.
The bakery is **next to** the supermarket.

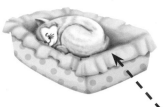

71

Nouns

Words such as 'apple', 'bedroom' or 'friend' are called **nouns**.

In French, all nouns are either **masculine** or **feminine**. When you use a noun in French, you need to know whether it is masculine or feminine, as this changes the form of other words used with it, like:

- adjectives (such as 'nice', 'blue', 'big') that describe it
- 'the' or 'a' that come before it

Nouns can also be **plural** (meaning 'more than one').

This dictionary shows you the French words for 'the' (this can be **le**, **la**, **l'**, or **les** in the plural):

- **Masculine** words are shown with **le** in front.

bag
le **sac**

- **Feminine** words are shown with **la** in front.

apple
la **pomme**

- In front of words starting with a vowel or sometimes an 'h', **le** and **la** become **l'**. So to find out if these words are *m*asculine or *f*eminine, look for a small '*m*' or '*f*' after it.

ambulance
l'**ambulance** *f*

- Plural words are shown with **les** in front, and are followed by a small '*mpl*' for *m*asculine *pl*ural or '*fpl*' for *f*eminine *pl*ural.

hair
les **cheveux** *mpl*

Most words in French add an **-s** at the end when there is more than one (in the **plural**). If the plural doesn't follow this rule, then this dictionary will give you the plural of the noun, in brackets. It is called an irregular plural.

animal
l'**animal** *m*
(les animaux *pl*)

Adjectives

An **adjective** is a 'describing' word (such as 'nice', 'blue', 'big') which tells you more about a noun.

In French, they mostly come **after** the noun ('a car black') but the spelling of the adjective changes depending on whether the noun it describes is masculine or feminine.

In this dictionary, you will find the **masculine** and the **feminine** forms, followed by an example:

black
noir, noire
a black car
une voiture noire

Verbs

Words such as 'eat' or 'make' are called **verbs** or 'doing' words. In French the endings in verbs change much more than in English, depending on who is doing the action.

Here are a few of the main French verbs:

avoir	**to have**	faire	**to do**
j'**ai**	I have	je **fais**	I do
tu **as**	you have	tu **fais**	you do
il **a**	he has	il **fait**	he does
elle **a**	she has	elle **fait**	she does
nous **avons**	we have	nous **faisons**	we do
vous **avez**	you have	vous **faites**	you do
ils **ont**	they have	ils **font**	they do
elles **ont**	they have	elles **font**	they do

être	**to be**	regarder	**to look at, to watch**
je **suis**	I am	je regard**e**	I look at
tu **es**	you are	tu regard**es**	you look at
il **est**	he is	il regard**e**	he looks at
elle **est**	she is	elle regard**e**	she looks at
nous **sommes**	we are	nous regard**ons**	we look at
vous **êtes**	you are	vous regard**ez**	you look at
ils **sont**	they are	ils regard**ent**	they look at
elles **sont**	they are	elles regard**ent**	they look at

aller	**to go**
je **vais**	I go
tu **vas**	you go
il **va**	he goes
elle **va**	she goes
nous **allons**	we go
vous **allez**	you go
ils **vont**	they go
elles **vont**	they go

have
avoir
*I **have** a bike.*
*J'**ai** un vélo.*

All verbs in this dictionary have an example to show you how to use them.

Index

A, a

acheter: **buy**

l'adulte *m/f*: **adult**

l'aéroport *m*: **airport**

l'agneau *m* (les agneaux): **lamb**

aimer: **like, love**

l'aire de jeux *f*: **playground**

aller: **go**

l'alphabet *m*: **alphabet**

l'ambulance *f*: **ambulance**

l'ami *m*, l'amie *f*: **friend**

l'an *m*: **year**

l'animal *m* (les animaux): **animal, pet**

l'anniversaire *m*: **birthday**

appeler: **call**

apporter: **bring**

apprendre: **learn**

après: **after**

l'après-midi *m/f*: **afternoon**

l'araignée *f*: **spider**

l'arbre *m*: **tree**

l'arc-en-ciel *m*: **rainbow**

l'argent *m*: **money**

l'argent de poche *m*: **pocket money**

arrêter: **stop**

s'asseoir: **sit**

l'assiette *f*: **plate**

attendre: **wait**

au revoir: **goodbye**

aujourd'hui: **today**

l'autocollant *m*: **sticker**

autre: **other**

avant: **before**

avec: **with**

l'avion *m*: **plane**

avoir: **have**

avoir besoin de: **need**

B, b

la bague: **ring**

les baguettes *fpl*: **chopsticks**

le bain: **bath**

le ballon: **ball, balloon**

la banane: **banana**

le bateau (les bateaux): **boat**

le bazar: **mess**

beaucoup de: **many**

le bébé: **baby**

le beurre: **butter**

bien: **well**

bienvenue: **welcome**

le bisou: **kiss**

blanc, blanche: **white**

bleu, bleue: **blue**

boire: **drink**

la boîte: **box**

bon, bonne: **good, right**

le bonhomme de neige: **snowman**

bonjour: **hello**

la botte: **boot**

la bouche: **mouth**

la bougie: **candle**

le bras: **arm**

la brosse à dents: **toothbrush**

le bruit: **noise**

le bus: **bus**

C, c

se cacher: **hide**

le cadeau (les cadeaux): **present**

le café: **coffee**

le calendrier: **calendar**

la campagne: **countryside**

le canapé: **sofa**

le canard: **duck**

la carotte: **carrot**

le carré: **square**

la carte: **card**

la carte postale: **postcard**

le cercle: **circle**

le cerf-volant: **kite**

la chaise: **chair**

la chambre: **bedroom**

chanter: **sing**

le chapeau (les chapeaux): **hat**

le chat: **cat**

le château (les châteaux): **castle**

le chaton: **kitten**

chaud, chaude: **hot, warm**

la chaussette: **sock**

la chaussure: **shoe**

la chemise: **shirt**

le cheval (les chevaux): **horse**

les cheveux *mpl*: **hair**

la chèvre: **goat**

le chien: **dog**

le chiot: **puppy**

le chocolat: **chocolate**

le ciel: **sky**

le cirque: **circus**

les ciseaux *mpl*: **scissors**

le citron: **lemon**

la clé: **key**

le clown: **clown**

le cochon d'Inde: **guinea pig**

le coiffeur, la coiffeuse: **hairdresser**

la colle: **glue**

coller: **stick**

comprendre: **understand**

la confiture: **jam**

le corps: **body**

le costume: **costume**

courir: **run**

la course: **race**

le couteau (les couteaux): **knife**

la couverture: **blanket**

la cravate: **tie**

le crayon: pencil

crier: shout

la cuillère: spoon

la cuisine: kitchen

cuisiner: cook

D, d

la dame: lady

dangereux, dangereuse: dangerous

danser: dance

le dauphin: dolphin

de: from, of

le déjeuner: lunch

demain: tomorrow

demander à: ask

la dent: tooth

le dentifrice: toothpaste

le dessert: dessert

le dessin: picture

dessiner: draw

deuxième: second

les devoirs mpl: homework

le dictionnaire: dictionary

difficile: difficult

le dîner: dinner

le dinosaure: dinosaur

dire: say

le doigt: finger

donner: give

dormir: sleep

la douche: shower

le dragon: dragon

drôle: funny

dur, dure: hard

le DVD: DVD

E, e

l'eau f: water

l'école f: school

écouter: listen

écrire: write

l'éléphant m: elephant

en bas: downstairs

en haut: up, upstairs

en retard: late

encore une fois: again

l'enfant m/f: child

ensemble: together

entendre: hear

envoyer: send

l'escalier m: stairs

l'escargot m: snail

et: and

l'étoile f: star

l'exercice m: exercise

l'extra-terrestre m: alien

F, f

facile: easy

le facteur: postman

faire: do, make

la famille: family

le fantôme: ghost

fatigué, fatiguée: tired

le fauteuil roulant: wheelchair

faux, fausse: wrong

la fée: fairy

la femme: wife, woman

la fenêtre: window

la fête: party

le feu (les feux): fire

le feu d'artifice: fireworks

la figure: face

la fille: daughter, girl

le fils: son

la fleur: flower

le football: football

la forêt: forest

fort, forte: loud, strong

la fourchette: fork

le frère: brother

le frigo: fridge

froid, froide: cold

le fromage: cheese

le fruit: fruit

la fusée: rocket

G, g

le gagnant, la gagnante: winner

gagner: win

le gant: glove

le garage: garage

le garçon: boy

garder: keep

la gare: station

le gâteau (les gâteaux): cake

le géant: giant

le genou (les genoux): knee

les gens mpl: people

gentil, gentille: kind, nice

la girafe: giraffe

la glace: ice cream

le/la gosse m/f: kid

grand, grande: big

grandir: grow

la grenouille: frog

la guitare: guitar

H, h

habiter: live

le hamburger: burger

le hamster: hamster

haut, haute: tall

l'hélicoptère m: helicopter

l'herbe f: grass

le hérisson: hedgehog

l'heure f: hour

heureux, heureuse: happy

hier: yesterday

l'histoire f: story

l'homme m: man

l'hôpital m (les hôpitaux): hospital

l'horloge f: clock

I, i

ici: here

l'idée f: idea

l'île f: island

l'infirmier m, l'infirmière f: nurse

l'insecte m: insect

J, j

la jambe: leg

le jardin: garden

jaune: yellow

le jean: jeans

le jeu (les jeux): game

le jeu vidéo: video game

jeune: young

joli, jolie: pretty

jouer: play

le jouet: toy

le jour: day

le journal (les journaux): newspaper

la jupe: skirt

le jus: juice

L, l

le lac: lake

le lait: milk

la lampe: lamp

le lapin: rabbit

se laver: wash

le légume: vegetable

lent, lente: slow

la lettre: letter

le lion: lion

lire: read

le lit: bed

le livre: book

le loup: wolf

la lumière: light

la lune: moon

les lunettes fpl: glasses

M, m

le magasin: shop

le magicien: magician

le mail: email

la main: hand

maintenant: now

la maison: house

malade: sick

la maman: mum

manger: eat

le manteau (les manteaux): coat

le marché: market

marcher: walk

le mari: husband

la marionnette: puppet

le matin: morning

mauvais, mauvaise: bad

le médecin: doctor

le médicament: medicine

même: same

la mer: sea

merci: thank you

la mère: mother

moins: less

le mois: month

le monde: world

le monstre: monster

la montagne: mountain

la montre: watch

montrer: show

la moquette: carpet

le mot: word

la moto: motorbike

la mouche: fly

le mouton: sheep

le mur: wall

la musique: music

N, n

nager: swim

la neige: snow

le nez (les nez): nose

noir, noire: black

le nom: name

le nounours: teddy bear

la nourriture: food

le nuage: cloud

la nuit: night

le numéro: number

O, o

l'œil m (les yeux): eye

l'œuf m: egg

l'oiseau m (les oiseaux): bird

l'ombre f: shadow

l'ordinateur m: computer

l'oreille f: ear

ouvrir: open

P, p

la page: page

le pain: bread

le pain grillé: toast

le panier: basket

le pantalon: trousers

le papa: dad

le papier: paper

le papillon: butterfly

le parapluie: umbrella

le parc: park

pardon: sorry

les parents mpl: parents

parler: speak, talk

le passeport: passport

les pâtes fpl: pasta

la peau: skin

peindre: paint

penser: think

perdre: lose

perdu, perdue: lost

le père: father

petit, petite: little

le petit déjeuner: breakfast

les petits pois mpl: peas

la photo: photo

le piano: piano

la pièce: room

la pierre: stone

le pique-nique: picnic

le pirate: pirate

la piscine: swimming pool

la pizza: pizza

la plage: beach

la plante: plant

plein, pleine: full

pleurer: cry

la pluie: rain

plus: more

la poche: pocket

le poisson: fish

le poisson rouge: goldfish

la police: police

la pomme: apple

la pomme de terre: potato

le poney: pony

le pont: bridge

le portable: laptop

la porte: door

porter: wear

le poulet: chicken

la poupée: doll

la poussette: pushchair

préféré, préférée: **favourite**

premier, première: **first**

prendre: **take**

prêt, prête: **ready**

le prince: **prince**

la princesse: **princess**

prochain, prochaine: **next**

propre: **clean**

le puzzle: **jigsaw**

le pyjama: **pyjamas**

Q, q

quatre: **four**

R, r

la radio: **radio, X-ray**

le raisin: **grapes**

rapide: **quick**

regarder: **look**

la reine: **queen**

rencontrer: **meet**

le repas: **meal**

le restaurant: **restaurant**

le rêve: **dream**

se réveiller: **wake up**

riche: **rich**

rien: **nothing**

rire: **laugh**

la rivière: **river**

le riz: **rice**

la robe: **dress**

le robot: **robot**

le roi: **king**

rouge: **red**

la rue: **road, street**

S, s

le sable: **sand**

le sac: **bag**

sale: **dirty**

le sandwich: **sandwich**

sans: **without**

sauter: **jump**

sauvage: **wild**

savoir: **know**

le savon: **soap**

le seau (les seaux): **bucket**

la semaine: **week**

sentir: **smell**

le serpent: **snake**

la serviette: **towel**

seul, seule: **only**

le short: **shorts**

le singe: **monkey**

la sirène: **mermaid**

le site web: **website**

le SMS: **text message**

la sœur: **sister**

le soir: **evening**

le soleil: **sun**

la sorcière: **witch**

la soupe: **soup**

le sourire: **smile**

la souris: **mouse**

se souvenir de: **remember**

le sport: **sport**

le stylo: **pen**

le supermarché: **supermarket**

la surprise: **surprise**

T, t

la table: **table**

le taxi: **taxi**

le tee-shirt: **T-shirt**

le téléphone: **telephone**

la télévision: **television**

la Terre: **Earth**

la terre: **ground**

la tête: **head**

le thé: **tea**

le tigre: **tiger**

les toilettes *fpl*: **toilet**

la tomate: **tomato**

la tortue: **tortoise**

tout, toute, (tous): **every**

le tracteur: **tractor**

le train: **train**

tranquille: **quiet**

le travail: **job, work**

travailler: **work**

très: **very**

le trésor: **treasure**

le triangle: **triangle**

triste: **sad**

troisième: **third**

trouver: **find**

U, u

l'uniforme *m*: **uniform**

V, v

les vacances *fpl*: **holiday**

la vache: **cow**

la vague: **wave**

le vaisseau spatial: **spaceship**

la vanille: **vanilla**

le vélo: **bicycle**

vendre: **sell**

venir: **come**

le vent: **wind**

le verre: **glass**

la veste: **jacket**

les vêtements *mpl*: **clothes**

le/la vétérinaire *m/f*: **vet**

la viande: **meat**

vide: **empty**

vieux, vieille: **old**

la ville: **town**

visiter: **visit**

vite: **fast**

voir: **see**

le voisin, la voisine: **neighbour**

la voiture: **car**

vouloir: **want**

W, w

la webcam: **webcam**

le week-end: **weekend**

X, x

le xylophone: **xylophone**

Y, y

les yeux *mpl*: **eyes**

Z, z

le zèbre: **zebra**

le zoo: **zoo**